The Story of Jesus has been created and produced by
HarperCollins*Publishers* Limited
77-85 Fulham Palace Road, London W6 8JB
© HarperCollins*Publishers* Ltd

Editor: Susie Elwes
Director of Photography: Michael Raggett
Photography: Tony May
Design: Schermuly Design Co. London

All rights reserved

First published in Great Britain in 1996

ISBN 000 197 945-0

Printed and bound in Italy

THE STORY OF
JESUS
Photographed as if you were there!

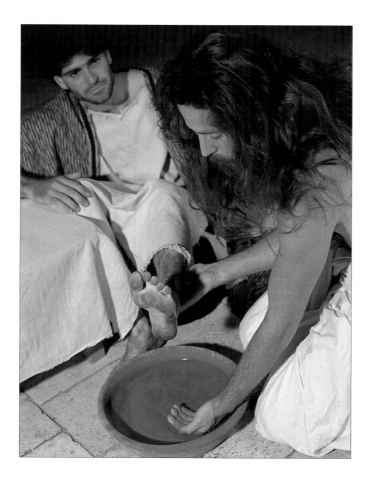

Henry Wansbrough

HarperCollins*Publishers*

Contents

Introduction

These few scenes from the life of Jesus give some idea of who he was. The stories are like 'snapshots' of Jesus as his first disciples saw him. The words used to describe the scenes are not always those of his first followers. The stories were first written down in Greek, the most widely used language of those days. But I hope the stories as I have re-told them give the sense of the originals.

The photographs are, of course, modern. But they were all filmed in the country where Jesus moved two thousand years ago. They include many sights and objects which Jesus himself must have seen.

Henry Wansbrough

The Birth of Jesus

Joseph was a carpenter. He and his wife Mary travelled to Bethlehem. Mary wanted her to have her baby there. It was the town where David, the first king of Israel, had been born. But they could find nowhere to live. The baby was born and Mary had to put him to sleep in a feeding-trough for cattle. Joseph named him Jesus, which means Saviour. They knew he was a very special baby who would save his people.

Some shepherds out in the nearby fields heard beautiful voices singing in the night. They were singing about peace over the whole earth. So the shepherds went into Bethlehem and found this new baby in the feeding-trough. They told Mary and Joseph about the singing.

Then some wise men came from the land of the rising sun to the East. They had read in the stars that a great king was to be born. So they brought Jesus rich gifts of gold and spices. But they also told King Herod at Jerusalem. King Herod thought this new young king would be a rival to him, so he sent soldiers to kill any young boys in Bethlehem. Herod had already killed his wife and two sons because he thought they planned to seize his throne. Joseph was warned of the threat to Jesus, and escaped with his family, south across the desert to Egypt.

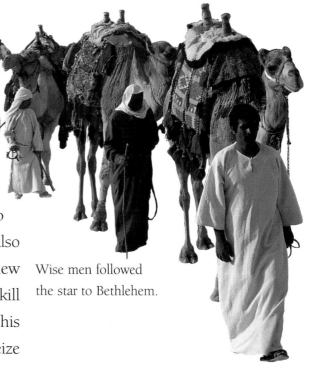

Wise men followed the star to Bethlehem.

Mary put her baby, Jesus, to sleep among the animals.

Shepherds cared for their sheep and lived with them all day and night.

The Young Jesus in the Temple

Every year Mary and Joseph walked to Jerusalem for the festival of the Passover. Passover celebrates the liberation of the Jews from captivity in Egypt, over 3,000 years ago. It is a sort of national birthday party. Whenever possible Jews would travel up to Jerusalem for the feast. For Jesus and his family it was a week's walk on stony paths.

When Jesus was 12 years old he went up to Jerusalem with his parents. For every Jew Jerusalem was the city of their dreams. Its centre was the Temple. It had 10 gates of bronze, so heavy that teams of 20 men were needed to push them shut each night. Above all, the

A high priest from the Temple. Men and boys listened to teachers in the courtyard.

Temple was the special dwelling-place of God, where people could feel his presence and be glad.

When the festival was over they set off home. But the boy stayed behind without his parents knowing. Jesus felt so much at home in the Temple that he forgot his mother would be worried. His parents thought he was somewhere among their friends. At the end of the day's journey they went to look for him, but could not find him.

So they went back to Jerusalem. Three days later they found Jesus in the Temple, sitting among the teachers, listening to them and asking them questions. Everyone who heard him was amazed at what good questions he asked and at the answers he gave. In her relief at finding him Mary said to him, 'My child, why have you done this to us? Look how worried your father and I have been, looking for you' Jesus replied, 'Why were you looking for me? Didn't you know that I was bound to be in my Father's house?'

The Rabbi or teacher has phylacteries, boxes containing the Law bound to his head and arm.

11

The Baptism of Jesus

Jesus had a cousin, John. John knew he had been sent by God to prepare people to be ready to greet the Messiah. They must give up their evil ways and reform. So he stood at the point where the main road crossed the River Jordan. Everything had to pass through the shallow ford, people, donkeys, carts. John called to them to wash off their sins, and change their bad habits. 'Prepare a way for the Lord!' he called. They must give up lying, cheating, stealing, quarrelling. John dipped in the river all those who listened and wanted to

Israel is very dry. It is woman's work to fetch the water from the well.

John baptised Jesus in the only river, The Jordan.

change. The Jews often used washing as a sign of washing away evil habits and starting a new way of life.

One day Jesus came to the River Jordan. John dipped him in the river like the others, though he knew that Jesus had no sins to wash away. As the two young men stood in the stream, Jesus heard his Father's voice ring out, 'You are my son. I love you'. Jesus knew that the great moment had come. He must start telling people that God's promises were true. All they need do was put their trust in him.

Jesus felt that the Spirit of his Father was with him, and would strengthen him. He knew that most people would not believe him. They would make fun of him, despise him, and would even torture him. But his Father's power would never desert him, even in death. His Father was sending him out on a mission as he had promised to Moses and his people, Israel.

Testing in the Desert

After his baptism Jesus wanted to be alone. He needed to think things out. So he went into the desert, by himself. In the desert it is completely silent. There are only rocks and dry sand. In this peace Jesus could feel the presence of his Father. His ancestors had wandered across the desert with their sheep and goats for forty years.

But he could feel the Power of Evil too. Three times Evil tested him. He grew hungry, so the Evil Power suggested he should change the rocks into food. He could eat and give everyone else as much as they wanted.

Jesus went into the desert to be alone.

The Evil Power suggested he should show off his power by leaping off the highest point of the great Temple of Jerusalem. He would not be hurt, for God would save him, and all the people would be amazed. They would be sure to accept him.

Finally he was tempted to worship the Evil Power itself. He could use Evil to attract people and confuse them. Then he could rule the whole world.

Jesus said, 'No' to the evil power. He remembered he was God's son. He could trust his Father. God had given him a task and God would help him. So he returned from the desert strengthened and secure.

Jesus Builds His Team

One morning Jesus was walking along the shore of the Lake of Galilee. On the beach was a little group of fishermen. Two brothers called Simon and Andrew were at the edge of the water, throwing their net out into the sea, hoping for a catch. He called to them. 'Follow me!' he said. Without hesitation they left their nets just as they were and followed him. 'From now on you will fish for people', he said. They did not know what he meant, but somehow they just wanted to be with this commanding stranger who had come into their lives so suddenly.

The three of them went on. A little further off he saw another group of fishermen. It was another pair of brothers,

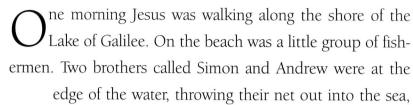

James and John, with their father, Zebedee. They had been fishing during the night, but they were still in the boat, mending the nets. 'Follow me! he said again. The two brothers just left their father and his men, their boat and everything they had, and followed him. They must have felt that Jesus was very special. They wanted him to be their leader. Jesus now had his little team of four. Soon he would build it up to twelve.

Many people still make a living by fishing in the Lake of Galilee. The Lake is 250 metres below sea level, so it is always warm. There are little villages round the shore. The fishermen set out at night in small boats. When the Lake is quiet they lay out a net in a large circle several hundred yards across. Then they pull the net together with a rope, like closing the mouth of a great sack. They hope there will be hundreds of fish inside.

James and John pull in the nets full of fish.

Jesus invites James and John to come with him.

A Wedding at Cana

Jesus was invited to a wedding in a nearby village called Cana. In those days people married quite young. The husband was often only 16, and the wife could be as young as 12. An older member of the family would be in charge of the feast. He would act as host. A wedding-party often went on for several days, and the whole village would be invited.

When Jesus arrived with his disciples, the wine had run out. This would be terribly embarrassing for the young couple. They had failed to welcome their family, friends and neighbours properly. Mary, the mother of Jesus, noticed and asked Jesus to help. At first he refused. But Mary simply trusted Jesus, and told the waiters to do whatever he told them. In the room were six huge stone jars, big enough for a child to hide in. They were full of water, so that people could wash before the meal. Jesus told the waiters to dip their jugs in these jars and take them to the host. When he tasted, it was wine, far better wine than the wine they had already drunk. There was a huge quantity, enough for everyone.

Most of the guests had no idea where this wine came from. The host asked the young bridegroom why he had kept back such splendid wine till the last. Mary knew, and so did Jesus' own disciples. They realised that Jesus was no ordinary person, if he could change water into wine in this wonderful way. It was a sure sign that God's power was at work in him.

Large jars used for storing water

A bride dressed to display her family's wealth.

18

A wedding feast
lasted for several days.

Jesus Teaches his Friends

As Jesus walked round Galilee, giving the news of God's healing, he explained everything to his special team of disciples. He used picture-language drawn from the country-side, to help them understand his teaching. He said his small group of followers was like a mustard-seed. It is the smallest of all seeds, but quickly grows into a large shrub. Or they were like yeast, which makes a small lump of dough swell into a loaf of bread.

He told his followers they were a light for the whole world: 'your light must shine in people's sight, so that they may give praise to your Father in heaven'. Following Jesus would not be easy. 'Foxes have holes, the birds of the air have nests', he said, but he himself had nowhere to lay his head. It was worth giving up everything to follow Jesus.

When Matthew came to write his gospel, he gathered together some of these teachings to give a picture of the sort of disciple Jesus wanted. This is called 'The Sermon on the Mount', because Jesus is teaching on a mountainside. At the beginning come eight blessings for eight special qualities. Two of these are: 'Blessed are the pure in heart, for they shall see God' and 'Blessed are those who make peace, for they shall be known as children of God'.

Jesus often told stories for his followers. One of his stories was about a sower, scattering seed by hand in his field. The birds came and ate up some of the seed. Some seed fell on stones and dried up. Some seed fell among weeds. The weeds choked the seed, so that it never grew. But some of the seed grew strong and produced a rich harvest. By the seed Jesus meant his own teaching. Most people took no notice of it, but his few followers were the rich harvest.

On a hillside above
Galilee Jesus taught
his friends and
disciples.

Jesus spoke to every-
one, even those who
were his enemies.

Jesus Heals the Lepers

Leprosy was a horrible disease. It hardly exists today, It flourishes where there is malnutrition. It begins with scabs on the skin, but eventually the sufferer's fingers and toes decay and drop off. Like many skin-diseases, it is very easy to catch. A person infected had to live separately, away from human habitation, and warn anyone who came near, by shouting out 'Unclean, unclean!'. Any normal life was impossible - unless the local priest certified a cure.

One day Jesus met ten people together, all suffering from the disease. They begged Jesus to help them. Jesus told them to go and show themselves to the priests, as though they were already cured. They trusted him, and as they went, they were suddenly cured.

We only know what happened to one of the ten. This one was a Samaritan, and the Jews hated and despised Samaritans. Samaria was the district between Galilee and Jerusalem, but people disliked it so much that they would go a long way round to avoid crossing Samaria. This Samaritan, finding himself cured, turned back again, praising God at the top of his voice. He threw himself down at Jesus' feet and thanked him. Jesus asked where the other nine had gone. Then Jesus helped him to his feet and sent him back to normal life.

Luke tells this story in his gospel to show that Jesus came to save all people, even the most despised and unpopular and handicapped. Jesus' own people did not bother to thank him. They just took the cure for granted. It was only the lone Samaritan who praised God so joyfully and said 'Thank you' to Jesus.

Lepers lived outside their villages. It was not safe to go near them.

The Good Samaritan

The Samaritan
poured oil and wine
on the wounds to
clean them.

One day a lawyer asked Jesus what he must do to gain eternal life. Jesus told him to love God above all things, and his neighbour as much as he loved himself. So the lawyer asked Jesus who his neighbour was. In reply Jesus told him this story:

A man was walking down from Jerusalem to Jericho and was attacked by bandits. The desert track between Jerusalem and Jericho is a very lonely, winding path between high cliffs. Robbers can easily set up an ambush, and there is no means of

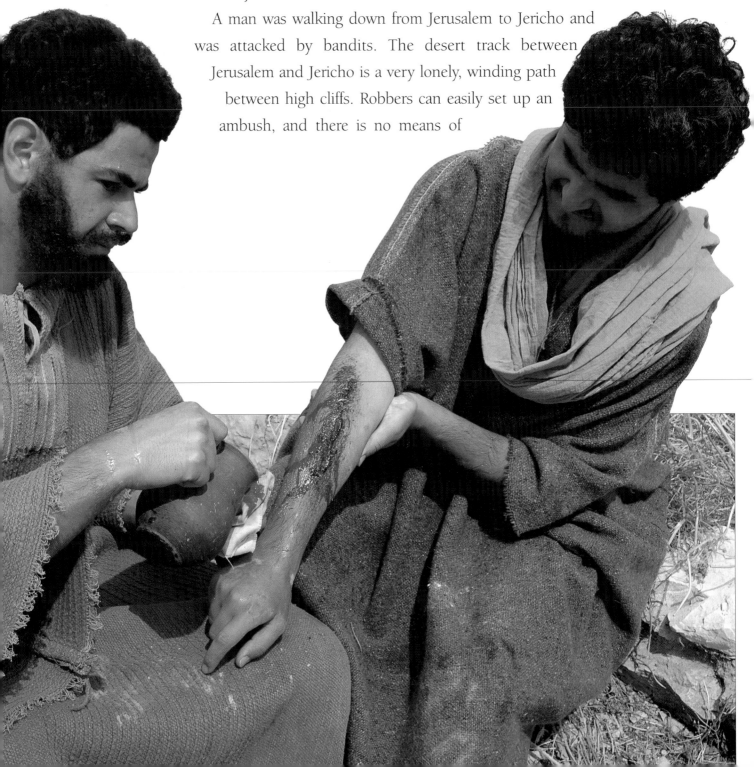

escape. They stripped the man and ran off, leaving him half dead. Soon a priest came walking down the same track. He didn't even go to look at the huddled body, but just walked on. Next another servant of the Temple saw the man, but he took no notice either. No one connected with the Temple was allowed to touch a dead body, and perhaps they were scared that he might be dead.

Then a Samaritan traveller came up and took pity on the wounded man. He went up to him, bandaged his wounds and put ointment on them. He put the man on his own donkey and led him to an inn and looked after him. Next day, as he continued his journey, he paid the innkeeper generously to go on caring for the wounded man. 'Look after him,' he said, 'and on my way back I'll pay for any extra expense you have.'

Then Jesus asked the lawyer which of the three travellers acted like a neighbour to the wounded man. 'The one who showed pity towards him', said the lawyer. It must have been difficult for the lawyer to admit that the despised Samaritan had done better than either of the Temple servants. Jesus told other stories to show that kindness and generosity are the most important qualities to make our own.

The Samaritan put the injured man on his own donkey and took him to an inn.

Loaves and Fish

Andrew brought a boy with some food to Jesus and Jesus provided a feast for everyone.

Late one afternoon the crowds were still following Jesus, bringing their sick to be healed, and listening to his stories. There were several thousand people there, and they had nothing to eat. By the time Jesus had finished speaking it was very late. The disciples asked Jesus to send the crowds away to get something to eat in the local farms and villages.

But Jesus was concerned for the crowds following him, like a shepherd for his sheep. They seemed to him lost and leaderless. So he replied, 'Give them something to eat yourselves'. The disciples thought this absurd; they had nothing like enough money to buy food for a huge crowd. They said sharply, 'Half a year's pay would not be enough to buy them even bread.' Jesus asked, 'How many loaves have you? Go and see.' Andrew, Peter's brother, went off and found a small boy with five pieces of bread and two fish from the Lake. He brought these along, and Jesus told the people to sit down.

Jews always thank God for their food before eating. So Jesus thanked his Father for the food, blessed the bread and the fish, and told the disciples to hand them round among the people. The disciples went on sharing them out till everyone had eaten as much as they wanted. Five thousand men, with their families, had enjoyed the party. The disciples picked up twelve large basketsful of scraps of bread and fish left over.

Hundreds of years before, when Moses had asked God to provide bread for the Israelites in the desert. God had given them manna. The people saw Jesus as a sort of Moses, and wanted to make him king. So Jesus went off into the hills, alone. Soon afterwards he told his disciples that he himself was the Bread of Life, God's own gift to bring life to the world.

Five loaves and two little fish.

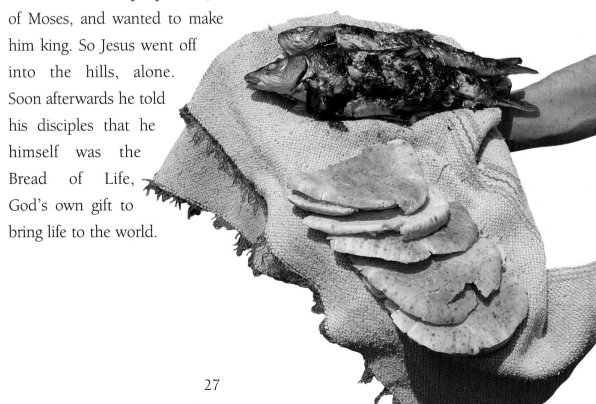

27

Jesus Heals a Young Girl

One day, as Jesus came ashore from the Sea of Galilee, a leader in the local Synagogue, named Jairus, came up and said, 'My little daughter is dying. Just come and touch her and she will be well again!' While they were still on their way to his house a messenger came and said: 'Don't bother Jesus. She is already dead.' Jesus said, 'Don't worry, trust me.'

When they got to Jairus' house they found people crying and wailing. 'Why are you all crying and wailing?' said Jesus. 'She is not dead. She is just asleep.' They made fun of him, but he went on in with her parents. He moved the mourners away, took the little girl by the hand and lifted her up. She began to walk around. Everyone was amazed at what Jesus had done. The girl was only twelve years old, and Jesus told them to give her something to eat.

The centre of every Jewish community was the synagogue. Everyone met there each week on the Sabbath (Saturday) to pray and discuss their Scriptures. The children were taught about God and His special care for them. The leaders of the Synagogue guided the service, and also made sure that any strangers or poor people were well looked after. The Sabbath was a great day for meeting friends and for lively parties.

When people died they were mourned with the sad sound of flutes. People cried and wailed even though they believed that good people would see God when the world came to an end. Jairus had gone on trusting Jesus' powers, even when he was told that his daughter had died.

When Jesus entered
the room the people
were already mourn-
ing the child's death.

A Story of a Father and Two sons

Jesus kept welcoming sinners and inviting them to join him at table. The Pharisees and lawyers complained. So Jesus told them this story.

A man had two sons. One day the younger one said to his father, 'Give me now all the money I will inherit from you when you die.' The father shared out his property between the two sons, and after a few days the younger son bundled up everything he had and went abroad. There he quickly spent all his money on wild living.

When he had spent everything a food shortage struck the whole country. The young man started to work for a local farmer, feeding pigs. He was so hungry that he would even have eaten the pig-food! Then he suddenly thought, 'I'm starving here, and my father's workers have plenty to eat. I'll go home, say I'm really sorry, and ask my father to have me as one of his farm-workers.'

So he set off home. His father was on the look-out, and from a long way off saw him coming. He ran to meet the boy and hugged him lovingly. The boy started to say he was sorry. But before he had finished, his father said to the servants, 'Quick! Bring him our best clothes and sandals. Prepare the food we had been saving and we'll have a feast.'

The elder brother was working in the fields and heard the party. His father left the feast and warmly welcomed him. But he was rude to his father, told lies about his brother and utterly refused to join the party.

The father ran to greet the son he thought was lost for ever.

Jews believed that pigs were unclean. To have fed pigs was a disgrace.

Jesus Brings Lazarus Back to Life

Jesus had some friends at Bethany, where he used to go and stay. They were called Martha, Mary and Lazarus. The brother, Lazarus, fell seriously ill. By the time Jesus got there, he had died. In the hot climate of Israel people are buried quickly, and when Jesus arrived, Lazarus had been in the tomb for four days.

A cloth covered the face and the whole body was bound with strips of material.

Mary was too upset even to move, but Martha came out to meet Jesus. 'Lord,' she said, 'If only you had been here, Lazarus would not have died.' 'Your brother will rise again', said Jesus.

'I know he will rise again at the resurrection on the last day,' replied Martha. Jesus said, 'I am the res-

urrection. Anyone who believes in me will live. No one who believes in me will ever die.' Martha replied, 'I believe you, Lord. You are the Christ, the son of God.'

Then Martha asked someone to fetch Mary. When Mary arrived she burst into tears and said, 'Lord, if only you had been here Lazarus would not have died.' Jesus was upset to see Mary crying. He gave a deep sigh, and wept too. He asked to be taken to the tomb. They all realised how much Jesus had loved Lazarus. Someone said, 'He gave sight to the blind. Could he not have saved Lazarus from dying?'

The tomb was a cave in the rock, with a stone to close the opening. Jesus said, 'Take the stone away'. Martha said, 'Lord, it is four days since he died. He will smell by now.' Jesus answered, 'If you believe, you will see the glory of God.'

So they took the stone away. Jesus prayed to his Father and then cried aloud, 'Lazarus, come out!' The dead man came out, his feet and hands bound with material, and a cloth over his face. Jesus said to them, 'Unbind him, let him go free!'

Many of those who saw this came to believe in Jesus. But from that day onwards the chief priests and Pharisees were determined to kill Jesus because they were jealous of his powers and of his popularity. They waited for a chance to have him arrested.

The ground was so stony that graves were cut into the rock and closed by a stone.

Jesus Condemns the Temple

Jesus overturned the market tables set up in the Temple.

At last Jesus came up to Jerusalem, the holy city. As he went through the city-gate on a donkey his disciples cheered and strewed a carpet of leaves in front of him, as though he was a king. Jesus went on into the Temple. This was his Father's house, where he had stayed behind as a child.

The Temple was busy with market-stalls and traders, people changing money and selling birds for the pilgrims to offer in sacrifice. Pilgrims had come from far and near to sacrifice at this great Temple, and to be at peace with God.

Jesus had to show that all this sacrificing of birds and animals was useless. Instead of killing animals, people needed to give their own lives to God. They needed to serve him generously. So Jesus began to upset the tables of the money-changers and the seats of the dove-sellers. He said, 'The Bible says my house shall be a house of prayer, not a market-place.'

Next day, Jesus began teaching in the Temple. The priests in charge came up and challenged him: 'What right have you to act like this? Who told you to do this?'

Jesus knew they wanted to stop him and would not accept him. So he questioned them in his turn, 'What right had John to call people to change their ways? Who told him to do that?'

All the people remembered John as a holy man, a messenger of God. The priests did not dare deny this. Jesus knew that if they did not accept John, they would not accept him. In fact the priests now began to look for a way of getting rid of him.

Money changers checked the weight of coins on scales.

The Last Supper

Every year, at the first full moon of spring, the Jews had a feast to remember the time when God freed Moses and the Israelites from Egypt. This was called Passover. The feast began with an evening meal.

On the afternoon before, Jesus sent two of his disciples to find a room for them all. He gave them a sign: it would be a man carrying a pitcher of water on his head - normally only women did this. They found the man and got ready.

Then Jesus and the others arrived. It should have been a happy occasion, all feasting together. But Jesus said one of them would betray him, even after sharing this special meal. They were all worried, and each asked Jesus if he was the one.

This special meal was full of signs. Instead of vegetables they had bitter herbs, as a sign of their bitter slavery in Egypt. The bread was unleavened as a sign of the hurried departure from Egypt. They drank red wine as a sign of the blood which had marked the doorposts of the Israelites in Egypt. The youngest person present asked the father of the feast to explain all these signs, though of course everyone knew the answers already.

But Jesus took the unleavened bread, and said, 'This is my body'. Then he took the cup of wine and said, 'This is my blood, the blood of the covenant, poured out for you.' Then Jesus told them, 'I shall never drink wine any more till I drink the new wine in the kingdom of God'.

After that he told them he would soon be taken from them, but he would always remain with them through his Spirit. They were full of dread at what was about to happen.

Jesus ate a last supper
with his disciples.

Jesus on Trial

Soldiers arrested Jesus as he prayed among the olive-trees in the garden. He knew they were coming for him. He was afraid and prayed to his Father for strength. One of his own disciples, Judas, led the soldiers. He kissed Jesus, as a sign to show them which one to arrest. They could not risk a repeat of his threat to the Temple. But they had to convince the

Pontius Pilate washed his hands to show he had no part in Jesus' execution.

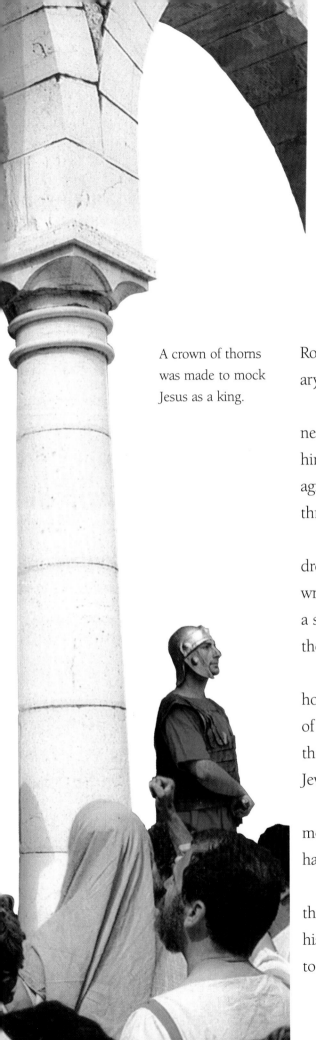

A crown of thorns was made to mock Jesus as a king.

Roman governor, Pilate, that he was a dangerous revolutionary. Only the governor could have him executed.

So the chief priests held a meeting. They tried false witnesses, but these could not agree. Then they questioned Jesus himself. Did he claim to be Messiah, so King of Israel? Jesus agreed that hereafter he would sit on the right hand of God's throne. That was enough.

During the night the soldiers made fun of Jesus. They dressed him up as a king. For a crown they put on his head a wreath woven from thorny twigs. In his bound hands they put a stick for a sceptre. Then they spat in his face. 'Hail, king of the Jews!' they said, and hit him with the stick.

In the early morning they hurried him off where Pilate was holding his court. They accused Jesus of claiming to be King of the Jews, and so a rival to the Roman Emperor. Pilate knew the charge was false. He asked Jesus, 'Are you King of the Jews?' Jesus replied, 'My kingdom is not of this world.'

Pilate wanted to release Jesus. But the more he tried, the more they hassled him. Then he had Jesus flogged. The whips had sharp metal spikes at the end.

Finally the chief priests threatened to denounce Pilate to the Emperor in Rome if he let Jesus go. Pilate would not risk his job. He washed his hands to show that he wanted nothing to do with it, and let them have their way with Jesus.

The Crucifixion

Then the soldiers took Jesus outside the city. They made him carry the wooden beam for execution. Beside the road they fixed him to the beam, lifted it onto a cross and left him there to die. Jesus even prayed for them. They were only obeying orders. The soldiers guarded him, so that no one could rescue him. All Jesus' friends had run away. Only some faithful women tried to get near him. His friends had come to Jerusalem with Jesus. The Roman Governor and the Jewish leaders in the Temple believed Jesus and his followers were a threat to them, so they accused him of being a rebel leader, and a sign, 'King of the Jews' was nailed to his cross. Everyone made fun of him as they passed, even the soldiers and officials.

On crosses beside Jesus were fixed two criminals. One of them taunted Jesus. The other asked Jesus' help, and Jesus promised him perfect peace and joy that day. Jesus hung for six hours on the cross. The sky grew dark in mid afternoon. Finally Jesus prayed one last time to God, his Father. Then he died.

Crucifixion was a cruel Roman torture for executing slaves. The executions usually took place beside a road, as a warning to others. People could read his crime on the notice fixed to the cross. With arms outstretched, a man could not breathe properly. The victim could hang there, dying slowly, for hours or even days.

Jesus was crucified between two criminals.

A Roman Centurion on guard.

The Empty Tomb

Mary of Magdala returned to find the tomb empty.

Jesus' body was taken down from the cross. In Jerusalem they used to bury people in an underground chamber cut in the rock. There was a flight of stairs going down, and then the door to the chamber, closed by a great round stone.

Three days after Jesus' death some women who had been among his followers went to the tomb. Perhaps they wanted to put sweet-smelling spices with the body to show their affection. Perhaps they just wanted to be near the body and grieve over it.

They arrived very early in the morning, To their amazement, the tomb was open, with the great round stone rolled to one side. Two men in blindingly white clothes suddenly appeared. These were messengers from God. They said, 'Jesus is not here. He has risen. Remember what he told you when he was still in Galilee'. Then they remembered that he had said he would rise from the dead. They were terrified.

One of the women, called Mary, just stood there and cried. Then she saw someone and said to him, 'Please tell me where you have put him'. She thought it was the gardener. The person said to her, 'Mary!', and she knew it was Jesus. She said to him 'Master!' and went to clasp him. But he said to her, 'Do not cling to me. I am going to my Father and your Father, to my God and your God. Go and tell my brothers'. So she ran off and told the disciples, 'I have seen the Lord'.

That evening they were all huddled in a room, scared, with the door locked. Suddenly Jesus was with them. He said to them, 'Peace be with you. As the Father sent me, so am I sending you',

The burial cloths left in the tomb.

The Road to Emmaus

That day two of the disciples were on their way to a village called Emmaus, seven miles from Jerusalem. As they discussed what had happened, Jesus himself came up and walked with them, but they did not recognize him.

He said to them, 'Why are you so depressed?' One of them, Cleopas, answered, 'You must be the only person in Jerusalem who does not know what has happened!' 'What do you mean?' asked Jesus. 'There was someone called Jesus of Nazareth,' they answered, 'a prophet. We hoped he would set Israel free, but our leaders had him crucified. What's more,

some of our women now say that he is alive again.'

Then Jesus said to them, 'Don't you see that it had to happen this way? It was foretold in scripture.' And he explained the prophecies to them.

When they came to the village they persuaded the stranger to join them for a meal. At table he took bread, said the blessing, broke it and gave it to them. No sooner had they recognized him than he vanished from their sight.

They set out instantly for Jerusalem to tell the disciples. But before they could say anything, the disciples said, 'The Lord has risen. Peter has seen him.' Then Cleopas and his friend told them how they too had seen Jesus.

Cleopas and his friend were joined by a stranger.